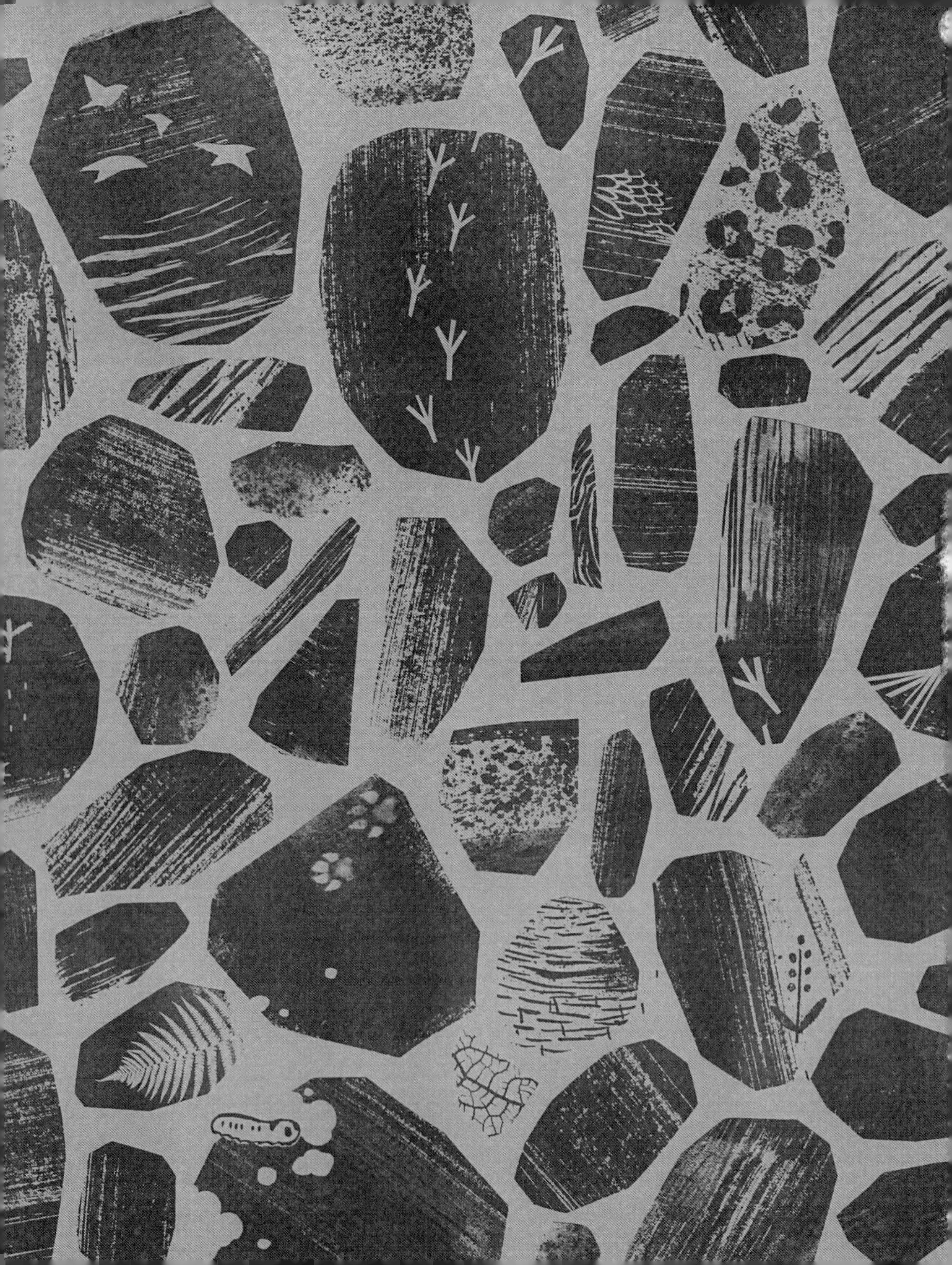

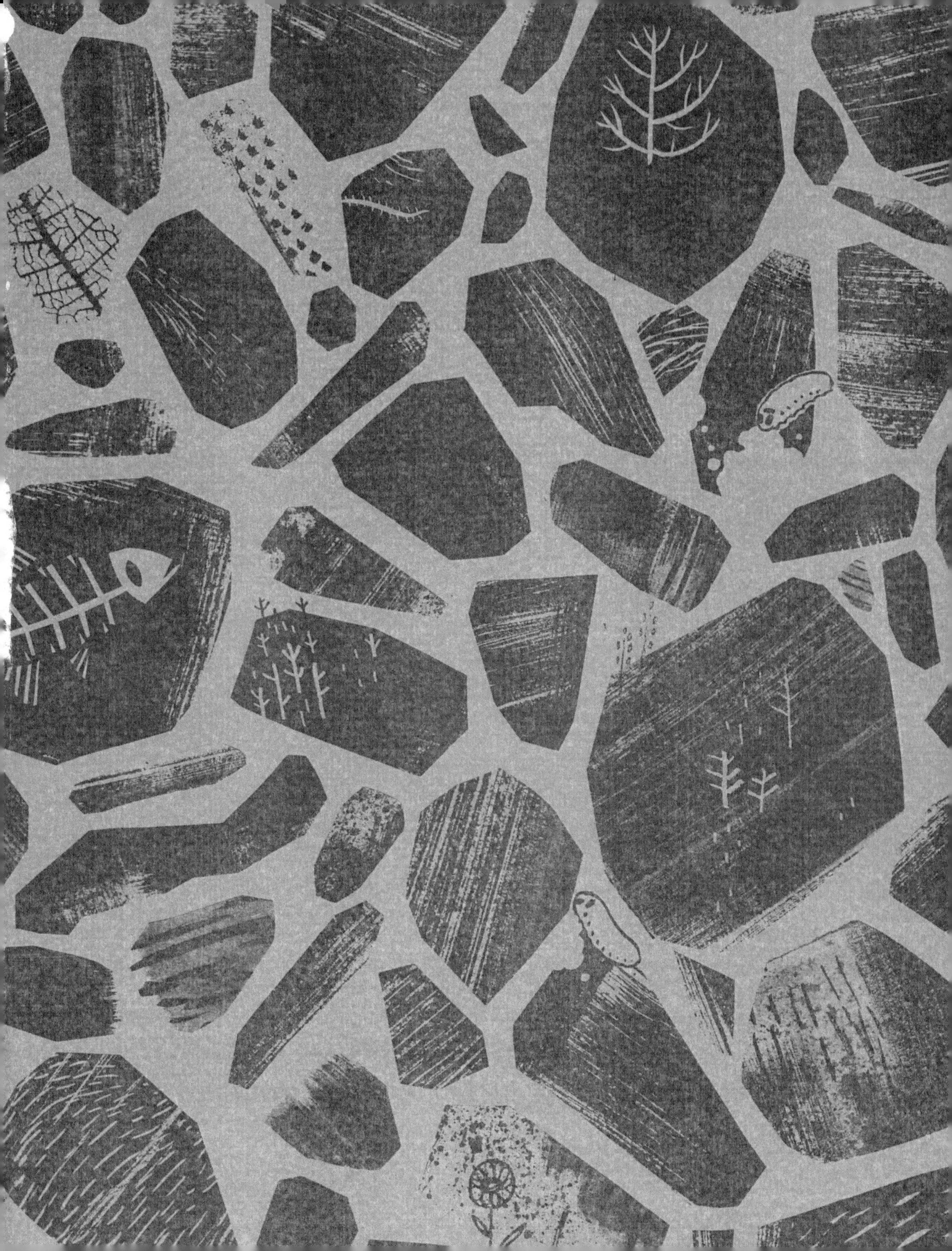

THIS BOOK BELONGS to:

The ALPHABET of ANIMALS and BIRDS

Prabha Mallya is an illustrator, writer and comic book maker. She is at her happiest when fussing around with inks and stubby pencils, and frequently has black fingernails. When she isn't drawing, she enjoys chasing cats over tin roofs, sipping *chai* on rainy days and reading graphic novels with no real panel flow.

You can read more about her work at her blog *www.crabbits.wordpress.com*

The ALPHABET of ANIMALS and BIRDS

PRABHA MALLYA

RED TURTLE
RUPA

Published in Red Turtle by
Rupa Publications India Pvt. Ltd 2014
7/16, Ansari Road, Daryaganj
New Delhi 110002

Sales centres:
Allahabad Bengaluru Chennai
Hyderabad Jaipur Kathmandu
Kolkata Mumbai

ISBN: 978-81-291-3121-8
First impression

10 9 8 7 6 5 4 3 2 1

In this book there are
More animals and birds
Than you'll see in a zoo
And many Special, Secret Words
Called ***Collective Nouns****, too.*

So, what is a COLLECTIVE NOUN anyway?

When you see a single bird or beast,
You can tell what you just saw—
The lion, **one** kangaroo, **an** elephant,
Or **a** rhino all alone.

Sometimes they come in pairs,
And threes and eights and forty-twos,
And scamper by so fast that
Counting them is no use!

You try to say that you just saw
A **few**, or **some**, or **more than one**
Lion or kangaroo or elephant or rhino;
But you can make it sound more fun!

A set of lions is just not the same
As a bigger, grander collective name.
So you let the lions decide,
And they call themselves a **pride**!

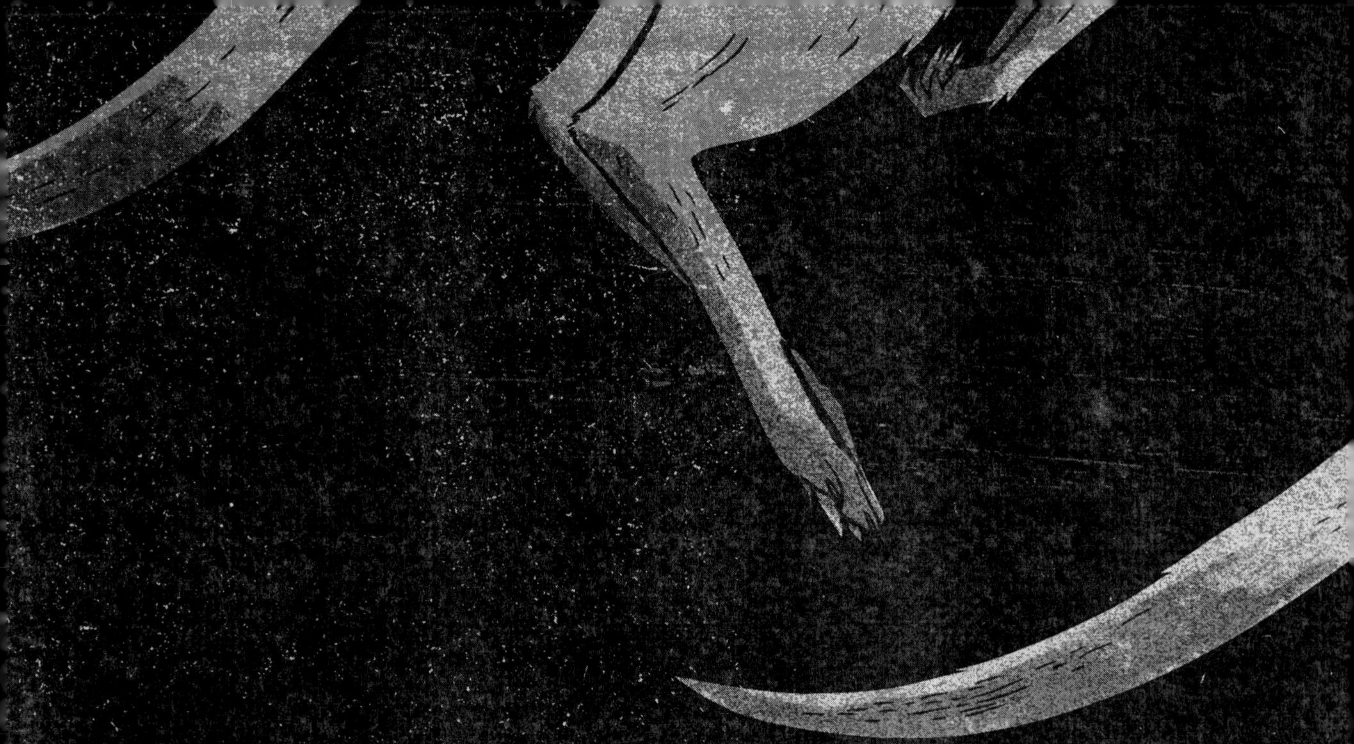

A group of kangaroos they could be;
But call them a **troop** and you might agree
They could look like a marching army.
Hippity-hoppity-hippity-hoppity!

You'll often meet a bunch of rhinos,
Stomping past the grass and trees.
Call them what they sound like, it really goes—
How about a **crash** of rhinos, please!

A crowd of elephants is called a **memory**,
For they remember everything, you see!
They know all those Secret Words,
Special Words for groups of animals, or birds.

They're called **collective nouns**—
Here's a book full of them.
Take it any place you go
And when you see more than one of an animal or bird,
You will know just the word!

a SHREWDNESS of APES
Aa
a SWARM of ANTS

Bb
a SLOTH of
BEARS

a
DISSIMULATION
of BIRDS

a SINGULAR of
BOARS

Cc
a MURDER of CROWS

a GULP of CORMORANTS

an
ASYLUM
of
CUCKOOS

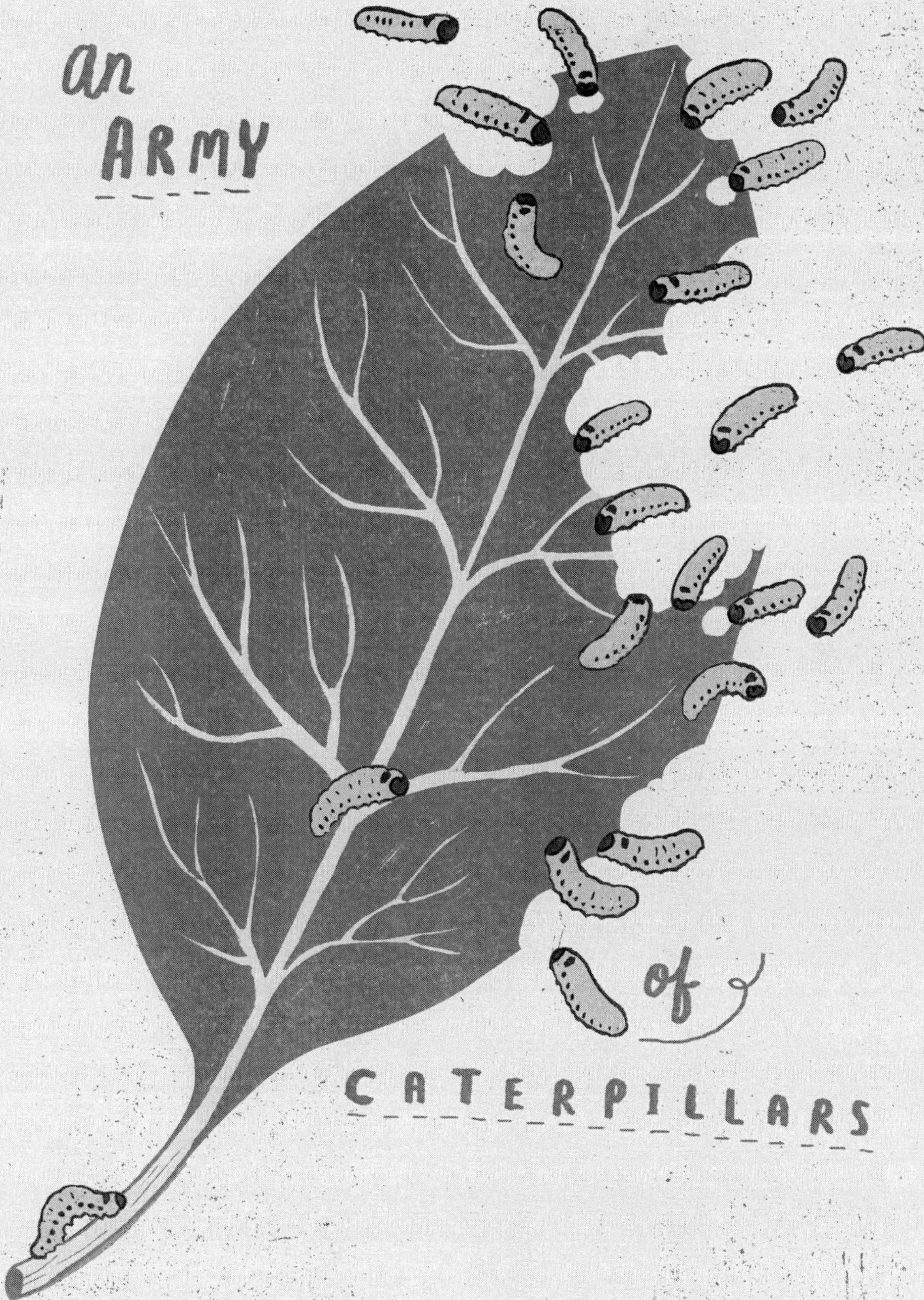
an ARMY
of
CATERPILLARS

Dd
a PADDLING of DUCKS

Ee
a
CONVOCATION
of EAGLES

a
MEMORY
of ELEPHANTS

a STAND of FLAMINGOES
a SKULK of FOXES
Ff

a
COLONY
of
FROGS

Gg
a
TRIP
of
GOATS

an
IMPLAUSIBILITY
of GNUS

Hh
a CACKLE of HYENAS
a BLOAT of HIPPOS

a MESS of IGUANAS
Ii

Jj
a
SMACK
of JELLYFISH

Kk
a TROOP of
KANGAROOS

a CONSPIRACY of LEMURS

a LEAP of LEOPARDS
Ll

a PRIDE of LIONS

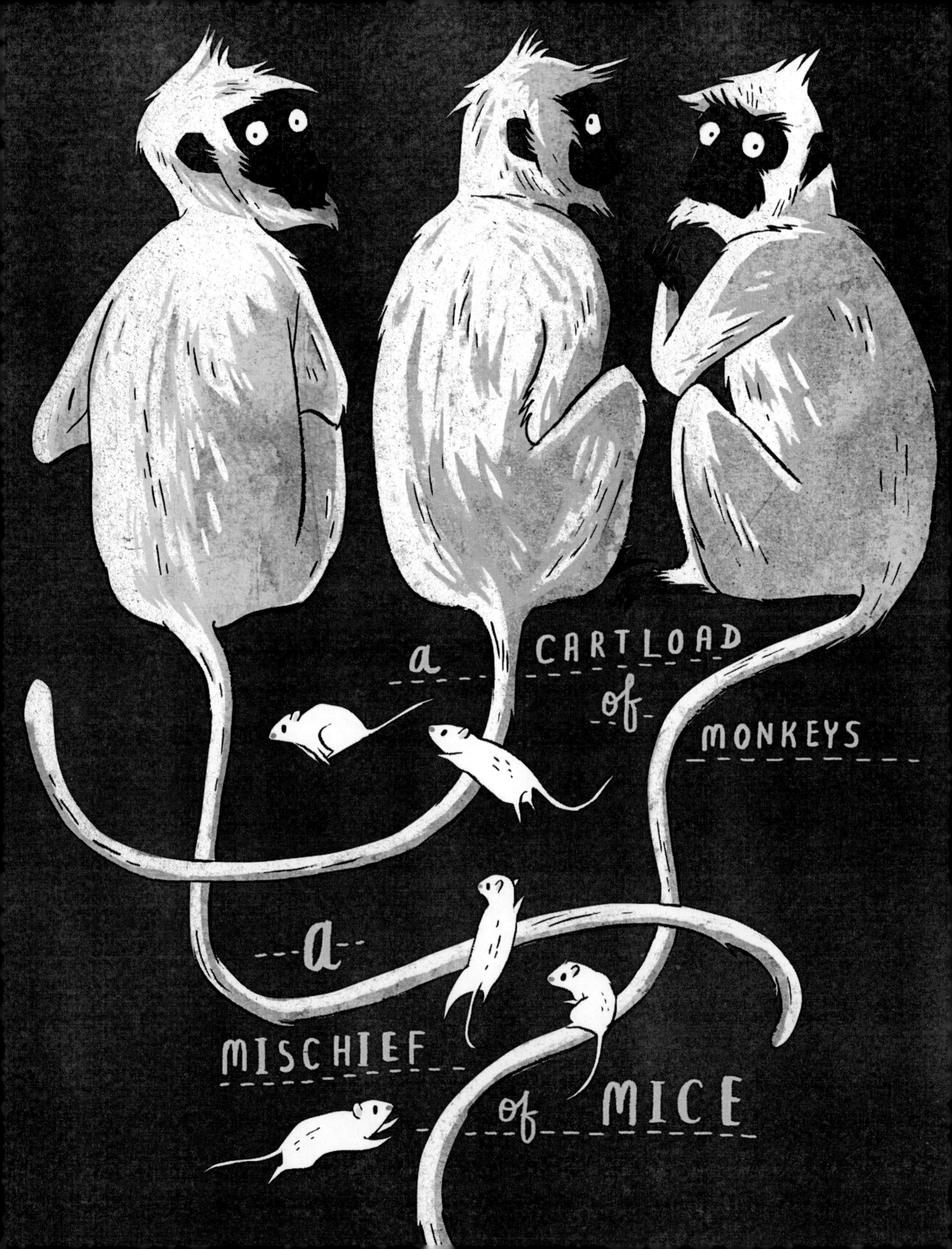
a CARTLOAD of MONKEYS
a MISCHIEF of MICE

a PLUMP of MOORHENS
Mm

Oo
Nn
a WATCH of NIGHTINGALES

a
PARLIAMENT
of OWLS

a RAFT of OTTERS

a SCOOP
of PELICANS
Pp

an OSTENTATION of PEACOCKS

a PRICKLE of PORCUPINES

Qq
a COVEY of QUAILS

Rr
a
DROVE of
RABBITS

a CRASH of

RHINOS

a SCURRY of SQUIRRELS
a WALK of SNAILS

Ss

a FLIGHT of SWALLOWS

Tt
an AMBUSH of TIGERS

a KNOT of TOADS

Uu

a BLESSING of UNICORNS

Vv
a
COMMITTEE
of VULTURES

Ww
a
HUDDLE
of
WALRUSES

a DESCENT of WOODPECKERS

a SCHOOL
of
X-RAY
FISH
Xx

Yy
a HERD of YAK

a COHORT of ZEBRAS

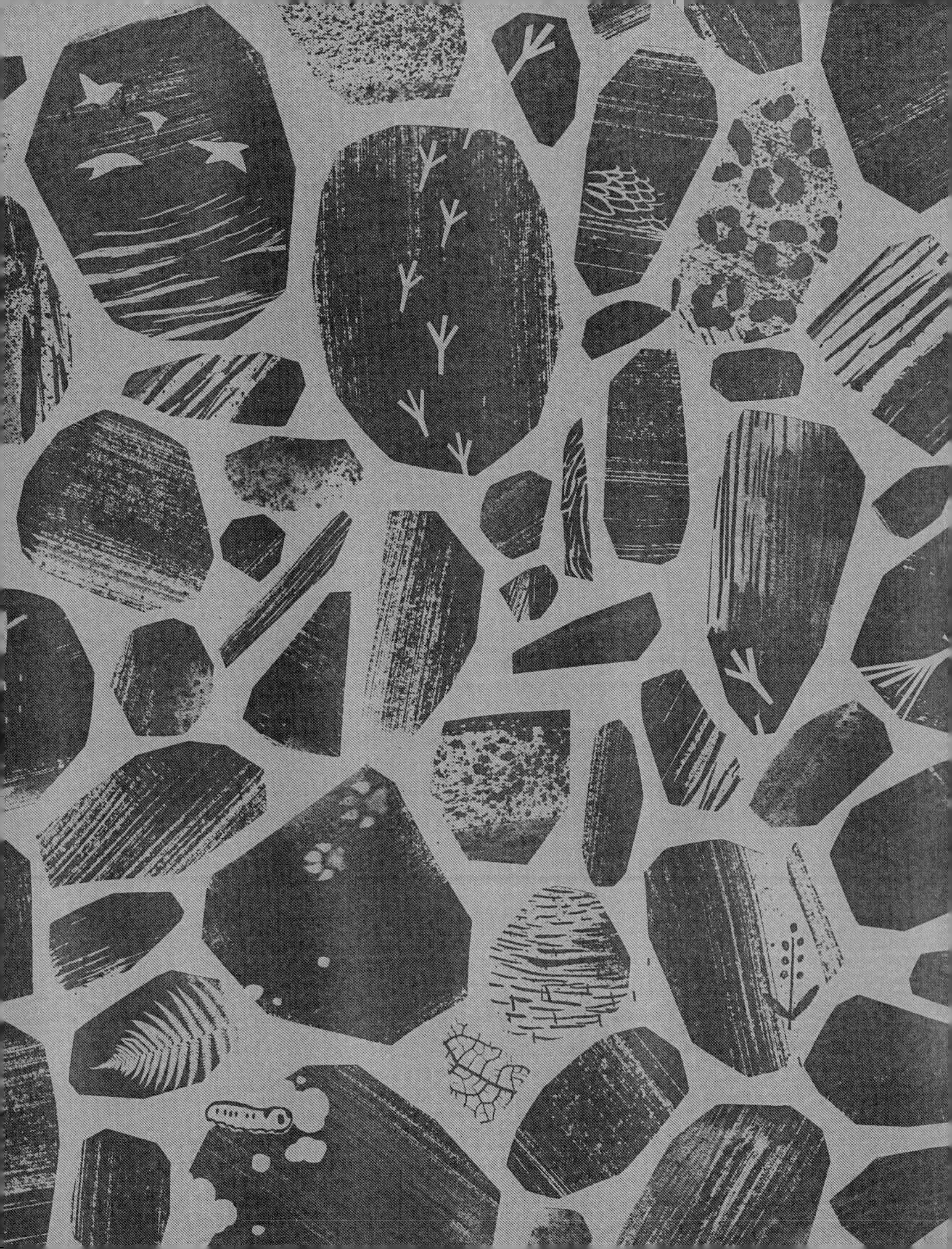

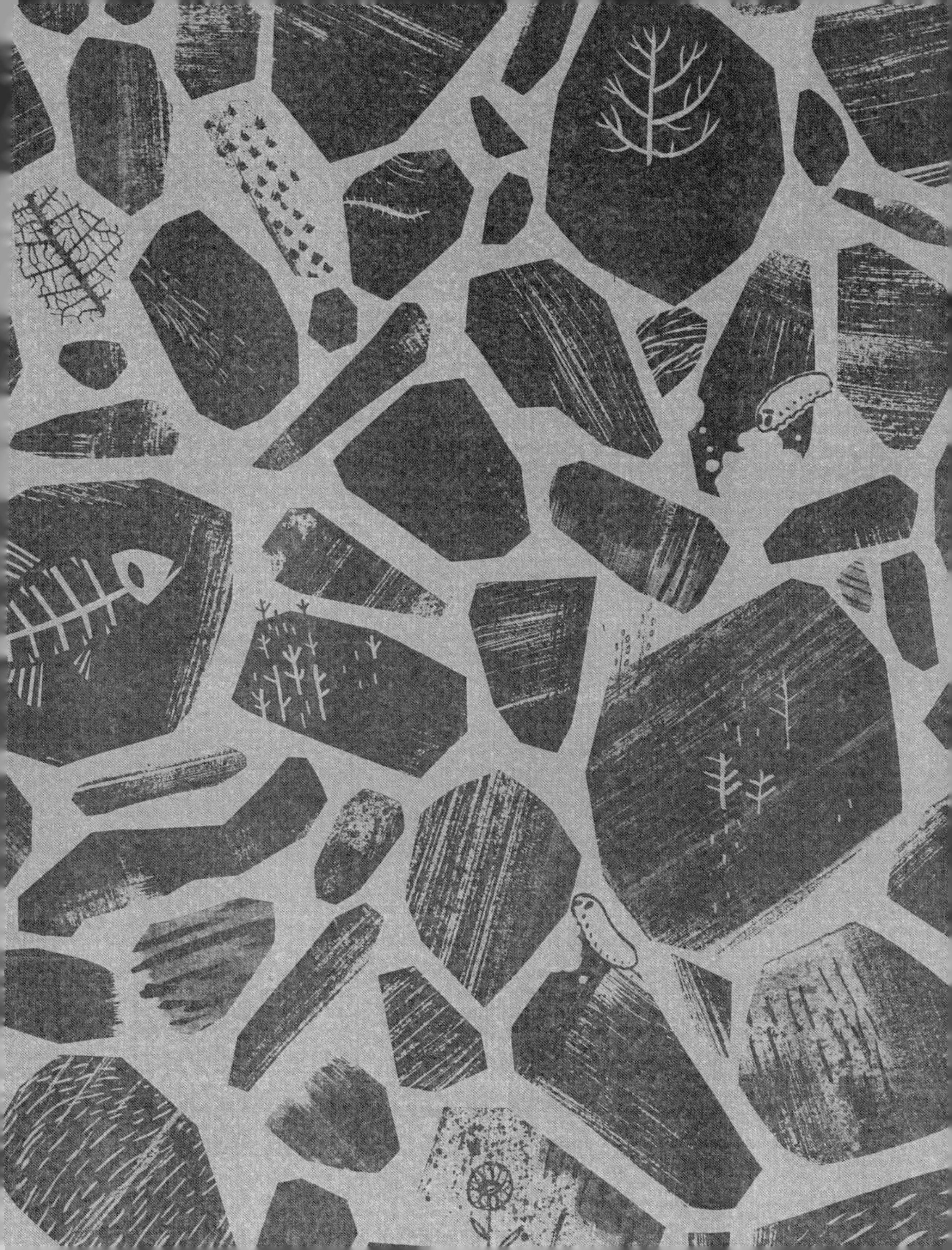